# 2018

© Juliette Publishing

First edition  How To Get Your Ex Back, Use Your Head To Fix Your Heart - The Heart To Head Method

ISBN  978-1-7200-3418-6

Text  © 2018 by Juliette Publishing. All rights reserved.

Cover Design  © Studio Ron van Roon

Website  www.hearttoheadmethod.com

Use Your Head To Fix Your Heart

# How To Get Your Ex Back

author Robert Faulkner

# About the author

My name is Robert Faulkner, 45, author of 'How To Get Your Ex Back – The Heart-To-Head Method', the book you are about to read.

Let me tell you something about myself. I have been in business since I finished university. First as a trainee, then as a manager, then as a board member in several companies.

Over the years I have learned a lot, in practice, but also from business courses: how to deal with miscommunication, pride, cultural differences and so on. The older I got, the more I valued helping other people, being their coach rather than their manager.

With this shift in my role, the issues changed as well: first they were strictly professional, but they became more and more personal, like relation problems – the issues that really bothered them.

As I could see that these issues also harmed their professional behavior, I tried to help as well as I could. I turned out to be good at it. 'Doctor Love', I was called and I regarded it as a compliment.

Then one day, five years ago, somebody said: 'Robert, I am incredibly happy with your advice. You helped me to get my ex back. I think that more people should benefit from your knowledge and experience. Why don't you write a book about it?' And so I did.

It is been a journey and it is funny, but looking back I see that all my past experiences somehow have contributed to the development of my method. Analyzed with the head, written from the heart – I wish you all the best,

Robert

# The Heart-To-Head Method

You want your ex back?

step one

feeling

# So You Want Your Ex Back

You want your ex back. It is possible and I can help you – as I have helped many others. In this book I will guide you through four steps that will get you and your ex back together.

# Heart-To-Head?

Heart-To-Head? Yes, that is right, because my method tells you to listen to your heart and to use your head at the same time: let them cooperate and get the best results.

This method hopes to bring you even more than the return of your ex. The Heart-To-Head Method wants to hand you the tools for you and your ex to build a better relationship than the one you had.

## HOW ARE YOU?

Do you feel as sad as you have never felt? So sad that you don't want to listen to the radio because every song makes you cry? Is there always something to remind you?

Do you call your ex several times a day? Do you never ever turn off your phone because then you might miss a call? Do you check your email constantly?

Are you thinking about your ex all day, what you should have said when you were still together, what went wrong, and what you will say when you might bump into each other? Maybe you don't want to eat at all but then sometimes you want to plunder your fridge?

So you and your boy- or girlfriend have recently broken up, and you want him or her back. You would walk a thousand miles, you would be happy to give away all your money, you would do anything, if that would help to win your ex back.

I know how you feel. I have heard the stories from my clients, but of course I have been through all this myself, more than once. I still can remember the pain, the sadness. It took over my life: I could not sleep at night, lost ten pounds in three weeks, at work I could not concentrate. On Fridays I would go to places I might run into her, her sister or maybe a vague friend. I would use every opportunity to talk about her, whether it be a taxi driver or a colleague.

I daydreamed about we would meet again, I fantasized that I would win her back because I was the one who would help her escape from a burning flat or out of the hands of someone bothering her in the streets. 'That's my girl,' I would say, 'get lost, punk, before I kick your ass.' She would fly into my arms, telling me how sorry she was to have ever doubted my love, she would kiss me and she would never ever leave me again.

A break-up is awful. Now, there is good and bad news. The good news is that in most cases it can be solved. Most cases, not all, because there are exceptions, off course: if the break-up is caused by domestic violence, abuse or serious alcohol or drugs problems, it might become too difficult to solve. In normal cases, research has shown that 95% of broken relationships can be saved and repaired. The bad news is that you have to work for it. If, however, you are prepared to do that, this might be the book for you: it will provide the tools, tips and tricks to win your ex back.

## IS IT SERIOUS, DOC?

Only recently has it become clear that it is actually a disease, to be taken seriously. It causes physical problems like stomachache, headache and nausea. Research has shown that people who suffer from deeply missing their ex-partner endure the same symptoms as post-traumatic stress disorder: irritability, problems sleeping and outbursts of anger.

The loss of a beloved one even causes a real medical condition, called broken heart syndrome: a traumatizing incident triggers the brain to distribute chemicals that weaken heart tissue. Might as well face it: you could actually be addicted to love. Cocaine cravings and love sickness stimulate similar parts of the brain. Recent studies shed new light on why it can be hard to control your feelings and behavior after being dumped – and why rejection sometimes leads to stalking, homicide, suicide and clinical depression.

## A TEST

So how are you feeling? How bad is it? Take the ten-question-test on the next page to find out. As you fill out the questionnaire, read each item carefully and mark the answer that best reflects how you have been feeling during the past few days. Make sure you choose one answer for each of the twelve items. If in doubt, make your best guess. Do not leave questions unanswered. This test is not meant to replace a clinical assessment but to help you judge how you are doing.

If your score is in the moderate or severe range you might want to talk to a counsellor or your doctor. If you are broken-hearted and sad, the chances are that you score in the range of a mild depression. No worries! That is normal, that is part of the disease.

## WHAT NOT TO DO NOW!

You are sad and hurt, probably angry, afraid you will never find anyone as special as this person, and you think that you have lost him or her forever. At this point it is fair to say that you are emotionally unavailable on virtually every level imaginable. In this state, you are not at your best and you are not thinking clearly and rationally.

Most people think the best way to get their ex back is to keep calling them and saying you miss them, love them, etc. The fact is that chasing your ex right after a break-up is only more likely to turn them away. The very best thing you can do in this stage is doing nothing. Stop calling him or her, no more emails and text messages.

You should use this time to think about what caused the break-up and what can be done about it. And at this stage, while you are emotional and desperate, the last thing you would want is to meet with your ex... Give him some space, give her time to miss you. Your ex is probably going through a rough time as well – even if he doesn't show that and on the outside appears all happy.

How much time? That differs from one person to another, but what is most important is that you use the time you need to become emotionally available and stable – ranting, raving, stalking, moping around and missing your ex does not help!

You cannot hurry love. Trying to put everything on fast forward is a big mistake that could put the process in danger! Just because you want your ex back so badly, doesn't mean he or she feels the same about you at this point in time. I am asking you something that may sound ridiculous, but you really should try it: accept the break-up. Try to see it as a good thing, think of it as a chance to improve your relationship – as has happened for so many people who broke up, who worked things out, got back together and became a better couple because of the break-up.

# Take this test to find out how you feel!

| | | A | B | C | D | Scores |
|---|---|---|---|---|---|---|
| | | No, not at all | No, not much | Yes, sometimes | Yes, definitely | |
| score points | | 0 | 1 | 2 | 3 | |
| 1 | I feel miserable and sad. | ☐ | ☐ | ☐ | ☐ | |
| 2 | I find it easy to do the things I used to do. | ☐ | ☐ | ☐ | ☐ | |
| 3 | I have crying spells, or feel like it. | ☐ | ☐ | ☐ | ☐ | |
| 4 | I don't enjoy the things I used to. | ☐ | ☐ | ☐ | ☐ | |
| 5 | I am restless and cannot keep still. | ☐ | ☐ | ☐ | ☐ | |
| 6 | I feel anxious when I go out of the house alone. | ☐ | ☐ | ☐ | ☐ | |
| 7 | I have lost interest in things. | ☐ | ☐ | ☐ | ☐ | |
| 8 | I get tired for no reason. | ☐ | ☐ | ☐ | ☐ | |
| 9 | I am more irritable than usual. | ☐ | ☐ | ☐ | ☐ | |
| 10 | I wake up early and cannot go back to sleep. | ☐ | ☐ | ☐ | ☐ | |
| score | | ☐ | ☐ | ☐ | ☐ | |

**Scores**

**0-10   Normal Life Mood**
You are in a normal life mood. Nothing to worry about!

**11-17   Mild Depression**
You are suffering a mild depression.

**18-24   Moderate Depression**
you are suffering from a moderate depression.

**+25   Severe Depression**
You are suffering from a severe depression. You might want to talk to a counseler.

*This test is not meant to replace a clinical assessment but to help you judge how you are doing.*

You can fill in the test online at www.youwantyourexback.com

# How To Deal With Heartache

It is a classic, especially among women: when feeling bad we have the insatiable urge to fill ourselves with sweets, chocolate and ice cream. Comfort food. But there are better ways to deal with it.

# Getting Out Of Your Cocoon

In his international best-selling book 'Healing without Freud or Prozac' Dr. David Servan-Schreiber explains how to cope best with these difficult periods or mild depressions. Some of the methods he advises are very useful when heartbroken.

Acupuncture, to start with, is an old and traditional Chinese treatment to relieve stress, anxiety and depression. Western research has demonstrated that stimulation with fine acupuncture needles directly controls key areas of the emotional brain. Secondly, make sure that when feeling down you receive enough light, preferably from the sun, and if not available from a special lamp.

A third suggestion is eating enough omega-3 fatty acids. Several studies have suggested that these acids are powerful antidepressants and can be found in fish, seaweeds, some green vegetables and in pills. You should eat healthily anyway, when you are sad: you are what you eat. Junk food makes you feel worse, alcohol is even a natural depressant: it increases the state you are in, not to mention the hangover.

## MOVE YOUR BODY!
But best of all to cope with gloom is physical exercise – even only twenty to thirty minutes, three times a week. Not only does it help to loose weight and to get in shape (so you will look better!), it has an incredible impact on your well-being, it works as effective as Zoloft, a modern antidepressant comparable to Prozac, because of the release of endorphins – chemicals that release feeling of euphoria and that block sensations of pain. Try to do the sport you like, make it a fun thing.

A great recommendation I would make, especially considering the situation you are in, is yoga, an amazing exercise. It not only gets you in shape, it also brings balance to your life – and not just for this particular situation you are in now. So why not go online and make an appointment with a yoga studio in your vicinity, today?

## THAT'S WHAT FRIENDS ARE FOR!
Sure, it is nice to have somebody to console and support you, and tell you everything is going to be okay. But even more importantly: you need friends to take your mind off of the break-up. This is what is crucial.

The distraction of going to parties, the movies, or just hanging out and talking is a great way to pass the time while you are in this phase. Going alone can be quite demanding in your emotional state. So even if you don't feel like going out with your friends or just hanging out with them, I urge you to give it a try. As a matter of fact, I am sure that some of your friends have been in the same situation that you are in right now and can provide you with some of the things that helped them along the way.

Think of it this way: would you rather be at home by yourself, crying and moaning about your heartache, with only yourself to listen to, or would you rather have some people that you care about on your side?

Talking to your friends is also a way to get out of your cocoon. You are in a very inward looking place right now, and hearing about what other people may be going through can put some things in perspective for you, and make you look at things more outwardly. You have been so fixated on yourself and what you are going through, that you tend to forget there are other people in this world – beside your ex.

Go on with your life, don't hide in your shell, stop moaning and try to have fun. Be nice to yourself, buy yourself a gift, visit a spa or – even better! – a health club. At first this may be difficult and the last thing you want to do, you may find you have to drag yourself out of your home, but you simply have to. It is the only way to get yourself off the road to nowhere, the vicious circle of self-pity. Act happiness, act confidence and you will find it becomes real. It is the old rule of attraction: focus on what you want and it will attract more of that.

And though this should not be your goal, think about it: what would impress your ex more? That she or he hears that you are doing great or that you are crying all day and night (unless of course you hope that your ex will come back out of pity for you).

In the meantime you should analyze what went wrong and work on yourself. This is not something that can be done overnight as it requires introspection, accepting flaws and the will to work on them. I will guide you through this process: it is Step One of the Heart-To-Head Method. What to say or do when you two meet will follow in Steps Two, Three and Four!

## YOU ARE NOT ALONE

Fifty-five percent of the people on this planet have suffered from love sickness, five percent of them during the last two years, no difference between men and women. So there have always been and always will be people suffering of heartache.

But there is something strange about the subject. While for any other disease, whether physical matters like a headache or a broken leg, mental ones like depression or burnout, an enormous amount of research has been done, piles of books have been written, cures and pills have been designed, heartache does not receive the attention it deserves. It is as if we think that it is part of life, something we have to endure and nothing really helps. And that is wrong.

I have found out that actually something can be done: it is possible to cure love-sickness, it is possible to win your ex back. My background in business made me look at the issue from different perspectives, I asked myself: 'Okay, little is known about the dynamics between two ex-lovers, but is this the only situation where two parties are having a fight? Where one wanted to get rid of the other? Where one wants to persuade the other to make up?'

Relationships exist between two lovers, but also between colleagues, between a company and a client, between two countries. All of these relationships sometimes deal with problems: countries may have been in war and have made peace again, one can hate a colleague, but somehow have to find a way to work with him. And look at business: when it comes to persuasion for example, we can learn a great deal from sales.

In these areas there have been done a lot of studies. In this book I tried to learn from them and transfer them to our subject: how to fix a break-up. In Step Two you and I try to analyze what had gone wrong. How did it end like this? Where did you go wrong? In Step Three you will learn to formulate what needs to be changed to make things right. In Step Four we talk about the next step: how to persuade your ex to come back to you and in Step Four we will discuss how best to get in touch with your ex and what to do when you meet him or her.

This may sound like a cold way of looking at your personal tragedy. But again, let me assure you: it is the best thing to do. Instead of only listening to your heart and your emotions, that tell you to call your ex, shout out that you miss her, you should rely more on your mind, otherwise you are going to make the same mistakes that so many people make. The very same mistakes that you hear other people make, that makes you tell them 'what in the world were you thinking!' Because that is the problem: they were not thinking clearly. Their emotions have gotten hold of them.

It is not that you are not allowed to feel anymore! Of course not. In this book you will be asked to look at the way you feel about your ex, yourself and your relationship and to analyze it: what you want is your heart and brain to cooperate! That is what the Heart-To-Head Method is all about...

Good luck!

You want your ex back?

# step two

# analyzing

# What The Bleep Went Wrong?

In this part we are going to do some analyzing. You and your ex broke up, but are you sure you know why? To draw the conclusions, We will be going back in time: your love life, how has it been? And how was the interaction with your ex? What can we learn from it? We will have a closer look at you. Yes, you!

# You are not alone!

What is it you could or should change in order to become a better partner? Furthermore, you are not going to do it all by yourself, you are going to ask a buddy to help you and give you the feedback only an honest friend is able to give you. This will lead to something very important: you know what you should do to make the relationship work.

As I said: you are not alone! In this book we will look at the stories of three other couples, each with their own problems. Different people, but with one thing in common: they want their ex back! I will use them as examples to illustrate the tools we are about to learn. Let me introduce to you:

# Ashley & David

Ashley is thirty-one, David is thirty-three. They had been together for seven years. After the birth of their daughter, three years ago, Ashley gave up her job, while David has devoted more and more time to his career, being an executive in a construction company.

Ashley became suspicious when David started working overtime even on weekends, a feeling that grew when she found out on David's Facebook-page that he and some girl were constantly openly responding to each other's post in a way that could best be described as flirting.

When confronted with this, David denied it at first, but then, a week later, all of sudden, he confessed: he and this girl were having an affair. 'But,' David said: 'I don't want to talk about it. I am leaving you.' So he left, taking with him only a little bag

with clothes and their small car. The first two weeks he lived at a friend's place, and then Ashley heard that he had moved in with this new woman – only three blocks away.

Ashley's initial emotion was that of anger. She felt betrayed, she felt furious about David's lust-driven and immature behavior. Her first impulse was to take revenge, she wanted to cut the sleeves out of David's shirts, she wanted to send an email to his friends and colleagues revealing his adultery – she did not, but instead gained five

kilo's by eating enormous amounts of Ben & Jerry's for weeks.

Then fear came up: how could she take care of herself and their daughter? David did not want to talk to her, nor their daughter. He just could not cope with the situation, he had not told his friends about the break-up, not even his closest ones. And next to fear came sadness and a determination: Ashley did not want this to happen; she wanted to fight for their relationship, for their family. She would not allow this affair destroy her life.

# Alex & Debra

Alex is fifty-six, Debra fifty-five. He is in sales, she is a teacher. They have been married for twenty-five years. The first years were super, then two kids demanded their love and attention, and gradually they realized that all the hassle and family life covered up issues between the two of them.

There seemed to be less and less time and interest for singing in a choir, discussing the books they had read and other hobby's they used to share. When three years ago also their son had left home it became painfully clear that they had little left in common – the fire of their relationship had gone out slowly... Dinners were silent, in front of the television, their sex life became non-existent.
Alex was the first to be aware of the poor state of their relationship and

tried to discuss it with Debra. But she did not want to, she said that Alex was exaggerating, making a fuss. Alex insisted and one night, when he had suggested relation therapy, Debra, normally quiet and reasonable, suddenly became angry. That night things had said between the two of them that should not have been said and ended with Debra shouting: 'You are right, our relationship is dead, so go, I never want to see you again.'
Now Alex lives in a rental

apartment close to work. Debra did not want to see him the first two weeks, nor did she respond to emails or text messages. When Alex came over to collect more of his belongings, she pretended as if nothing had happened, she was polite and formal, almost as if he were a stranger.

Alex was sad: he still believed in their relationship and wanted to fight for it.

# Suzy & Mike

Suzy is twenty-three, Mike twenty-five. They had met in College, and had moved in together right after graduation. Their life was great, they had a lot of fun, they were soul mates so it seemed. But as their relationship became more serious, problems arose.

Mike was from Asian origin and his family was very important to him. He wanted Suzy to participate in their birthday parties, gatherings and holidays, but Suzy somehow felt she was an outsider. She had the impression that Mike's family preferred a girl with similar background. No matter how hard she tried, the gap became more significant.

For Mike this was devastating: he felt torn between two worlds. He really loved Suzy, but at the same time he felt the pressure of his family demanding loyalty to their values. Finally, after six months of struggle, he broke up with her.

Mike left and returned to live with his family. Suzy was sad and tired after all the effort. She also felt it was unfair and that this should not be a reason for ending such a great relationship. She wanted Mike back and decided to fight for it.

# Common Reasons For Break-up

One of the most important things you want to take away from writing this Love Résumé is to determine the real reason for the break-up with your ex. Sometimes it is clear, but in most cases you are guessing, either because your ex was not able to tell you or because you know that the mentioned reason is not the deeper cause. But what is the real cause?

# Finding The True Cause

I listed some frequently cited reasons for causing a break-up:

PHYSICAL
- Sexual incompatibility
- Infidelity
- Falling out of love

PERSONALITY
- Inability to solve quarrels or irritations.
- Inability to accept each other's petty idiosyncrasies.
- Lack of maturity.
- Intellectual incompatibility.
- Flaws in communication.

CULTURE AND LIFESTYLE
- Insistence of sticking to traditional roles.
- Religious beliefs or religious conversion.
- Lack of room for individual growth.
- Differences in personal and career goals.
- Different expectations about household tasks.
- Financial problems.
- Interference from in-laws or parents.
- Different expectations about having children.

OTHER
- Lack of commitment to the relationship.
- Abandonment, whether or not temporary.

Eighty percent chance that the cause(s) for your break-up can be found on the list! In general you see that most of them show overlap and are interwoven. I recommend you to use them as an easy reference, to get your thought process going. But remember: you know best what happened...

## MEN ARE FROM MARS, WOMEN ARE FROM VENUS!

To find out what went wrong and to gauge the frustrations that may exist on both sides, it is good to stop and think for a moment about the differences between men and women. They are obvious, but still men mistakenly expect women to think and communicate and react the way men do, and women expect men to think and communicate and react the way women do.

What are these differences about? They concern priorities, perspectives, way of communication, and basic desires.

Well, to name a few: men get their sense of self from achievement. They are task-oriented, and being self-reliant is very important to them. Asking for help is an admission of failure, a weakness. Men usually are goal focused, while women tend to enjoy the process.

Not that reaching a goal is not important, but they like the getting there too. You can see this when a man and a woman are driving to their holiday destinations: men want to get there as soon as possible, while women want to treasure the time talking and maybe stop at the outlet malls along the way.

Men are competitive, they want to win, they want to prove themselves, while women tend to be cooperative. Men are logical, women are intuitive. Men can only focus on one thing at a time: they cannot talk to their wives and watch television at the same time. Women can multi-task. Men are action-oriented, women tend to talk.

For men words are words, simply for conveying facts and information. But for women, words mean much more. They help them to feel better when they are upset, it is a way to create intimacy. To a woman, words are almost like breathing! Sounds familiar?

For men admiration is really important. And you know how things go: in the beginning of a relationship all is rosy. A girl is not laughing at her boyfriend's jokes like she used to. She is not getting all dressed up as much as she used to for him. She is probably not as affectionate as she once was. Most men don't cheat on their girlfriend or wife because they found somebody sexier or prettier. The real reason is often that they feel that their girlfriend or wife doesn't admire them like in the old days... So when they meet somebody who is laughing at their jokes, and who is being affectionate to him, it is something that touches them on a deep level – something that is probably lacking in the relationship they are in.

Men tend not to tell their women about this: they are too stubborn for that. They also don't want to deal with any confrontations. Instead of sitting down and talking about it, men prefer to avoid the issue.

Women, on the other hand, need the appreciation. Women, in nature, are usually loyal, but that changes when they no longer feel appreciated by their man. For men this is difficult to grasp, because most of the time it is not even a case of attention, it is in showing appreciation for all the little things that she does.

Women want to feel more valued and respected in the relationship. Another important factor is the 'friendship' aspect of the relationship. The fact that you are not only lovers, but also friends usually means more to a woman than it does to a man.

A woman wants to be able to talk to her man, in the same manner she should be able to talk to one of her girlfriends.

She wants to know that you care about how she is feeling, and what is going on with her life, whether it be her job, relationships, etc.

Another difference between men and women regarding relationship is how they see infidelity. Research has shown that most men become much more jealous about sexual infidelity than they do about emotional infidelity, while women feel the opposite.

## WHAT ABOUT MASLOW?

Another way to look at the cause for your break-up is through the pyramid of needs, identified by one of the first modern psychology professors, Abraham Harold Maslow. Maslow listed different levels of needs, in a standard order of importance.

The most essential needs are listed at the bottom, and so forth. The idea is that an individual cannot be at the next level, unless all needs below have been fulfilled. The needs mentioned by Maslow

may help you to explain for yourself what happened. So ask yourself: were one or more of the needs perhaps not fulfilled?

At the bottom of the pyramid are the elementary needs of a human being: food, water and sex. These are typically the biological needs to live, to survive and to propagate.

The next level consists of needs like: security, order, and stability. These are typically the needs for feeling safe and protected. Think about a home, insurance, steady income and so forth.

Once people have basic nutrition, shelter and safety, they attempt to accomplish more. The third level of need is 'Belonging and Love', psychological needs: when individuals have taken care of themselves physically, they are ready to share themselves with others. So one needs to belong to a group, to be accepted by others, to feel love and affection.

The fourth level is achieved when individuals feel comfortable with what they have accomplished. This is the 'esteem'-level, the level of success and status (from self and others). It is about the need

*What needs are fulfilled you reckon?*

to be recognized and approved, to achieve and reach
something that is respected by others, to be perceived
as competent.

I summarize a few needs that may be extra
relevant to you:
- feeling safe & protected
- living a structured life
- belonging to a group
- being accepted by others
- being loved; feeling intimacy
- to achieve; being respected
- developing oneself

Where these fulfilled on both sides you reckon?

Now that you have taken a look at the frequently
cited reasons for causing a break-up and studied the
different layers of individual needs, it is time for you
to look up the Love Résumé at the end of this book
and spend a couple of hours thinking and writing.

Good luck!

# Those that fail to learn from history

are doomed to repeat it

*Winston Churchill*

# Why Tell Me Why — A Love Résumé?

Alex and Debra ended their relationship in a fight, yelling nasty things at each other. Alex left their house and went to live in a rental flat, having all the time of the world to think: 'What had happened? Why?' Because this was the last thing he wanted when he urged Debra to talk about their life and love, their complaints, hopes and expectations. But what had really happened? What is the true cause of their break-up?

# Writing A Love Résumé

*"Good, it is supposed to be – Make it as personal as you can. Believe me, you cannot imagine a feeling everyone hasn't had. Make it personal, tell the truth, and then write 'Burn this' on it." – Lanford Wilson, Burn This.*

A useful tool to understand the reasons why things have happened is to write a Love Résumé. We all know what a résumé is, whether it was to apply for a job, or to get accepted at a school: we all have produced one at some point in our lives. You write down your education and past jobs and you add in short what it has meant to you.

Now I would like you to do the same, not looking at your professional life, but at your private life. It helps you to get a clear picture of your past and maybe to see patterns and connections. Remember: life is lived forwards and understood backwards!

My advice: be honest when filling in your Love Résumé! This goes for all the exercises in this book. Try to look at your past with an open mind and fresh eyes, also at the things that have gone wrong. This may shed new light: maybe you will come to a conclusion that you have made mistakes. That is okay. Everybody makes them, nobody is perfect. As a wise man once said: you are perfect within your imperfection.

Blaming others, your ex-partners, other people or the universe itself doesn't help. But if you have the courage to stand up and admit, even to yourself, that you too contributed to the problems in past relationships, in some small or large way, you start to see a new way instead of being stuck in the past. And just as you learn when to not fall into the same hole when you are walking around the block, you have more chance of success when you can avoid the same mistakes next time round.

At the end of the book you will find a Love Résumé as an appendix. I would like you to fill in two: one for you and one for your ex. The one for your ex may be a bit difficult, but give it try and see how useful it is to see things through her or his eyes.

Treat this filling in as if it was an assignment for work. Try to leave all the emotions out of it, and focus strictly on the facts. This is obviously not going to be as much fun, but you have to be mature about this. Don't say one of the things that went wrong was that 'he was a schmuck' or 'she was a @#&@'. That is not going to solve anything. Try to dig a little deeper and see what you find.
When it comes to a break-up, it was either a gradual thing, where a lot of little problems just became too

# open honest critical receptive humble introspective

much to handle or it was a one-time deal breaker that caused the relationship to end. Either way, you have to treat this respectfully.

When it comes to finding the negative aspects, it could be something like having different ideas of what your future would be, loss of physical attraction, somebody wanted children and the other did not. Obviously, it is going to be different for each person, but try to be specific.

## WORD CLOUD

I have prepared a simple word cloud to bring you in the mood for this exercise. Concentrate, look at the words and try to get the desired mind-set: When

filling in your Love Résumé you may find that only a couple of things went wrong, or a whole laundry list. When you get them all out, you will look at your relationship as a project that needs some retooling, and you will know what kind of work has to be done.

On the subject of cheating, if this is the reason why the break-up took place, either by you or your ex, it is usually something deeper. Even if it feels like an isolated incident, I am sure there was something under the surface that caused it!

'Let's do it!', as an example I will show you Ashley's Love Resume on the next page.

# Ashley's Love Résumé

## OUR MEETING AND BREAK-UP IN DETAIL

### MEETING AND FIRST KISS

We met at a two-day business training, when David was still with Karen, his ex. He asked my mobile number with a lame excuse, we had lunch the next week. Our first kiss was – how cheesy! – in the movies.

### BREAKING UP

David is having an affair. I found out and confronted David, at first he denied it. A week later he confessed, but did not want to talk about it. In an email he wrote to me that he thought that he and I don't fit together anymore, that we have grown apart.

## ASHLEY: EXPERIENCES

### THE WORST EXPERIENCE

- When I found out about David and this girl, whose name I won't mention. He is been living a secret life.
- On my 30th birthday he had to be in Atlanta for a business meeting, he did not want to reschedule.
- He has insulted my best friends at several occasions, by not showing up or leaving halfway during dinner.

### THE BEST EXPERIENCE

- The birth of our daughter: David was really sweet then.
- Our holidays, especially the one in Mexico in 2009.
- Last year he completely surprised us with a weekend away.

## ASHLEY: EDUCATION

*Boyfriends prior to ex. Who broke up and what was the reason?*

- Phil was my high school sweetheart. I cannot remember how we broke up!
- Christian was my first serious boyfriend, but I broke up with him when he turned out to sweet.
- John, whom I also met at work. I broke up with him, when I caught him cheating with his secretary.

## ASHLEY: SKILLS

*List your two skills that are the most and the least beneficial to a relationship.*

### MOST BENEFICIAL

- Our house is really a home!
- I tend to look at the bright side

### LEAST BENEFICIAL

- According to David I am not very flexible
- Maybe I have grown too much of a stay-at – usually! – home…

## DAVID: EXPERIENCE

THREE WORST EXPERIENCES WITH ME

• I think that for David his worst experience was the moment I confronted him with the other woman. I guess this is what he feared most, and that is why he kind of froze.
• I remember that I really disappointed David when I did not want to join him to a supposedly glamorous business dinner.
• I cannot come up with a third one...

THREE BEST EXPERIENCES WITH ME

• The birth of our daughter: David was really sweet then.
• Our holidays, especially the one in Mexico in 2009.
• He always told me absolutely adored my cooking, especially the special dinners I made every month (French or Italian).

## DAVID: EDUCATION

*Girlfriends prior to ex. Who broke up and what was the reason?*
• Donna was his first love. I don't know how they broke up. I know it has been difficult for him at that time, but he doesn't talk much about these matters.
• Jacky, a girl he met at work. She was married at the time, she and David were seeing each other. David dumped her.
• Karen, the one he was with when we met...

## DAVID: SKILLS

*List your two skills that are the most and the least beneficial to relationship*
Most beneficial
• He brings in the money...
• He is funny!

LEAST BENEFICIAL

• I wish he would share his feelings more often
• He is obviously a good liar

*You can download a template résumé from www.youwantyourexback.com*

# Find A Buddy

By now you will have prepared your first
Love Résumé. Well done! But it is only a start:
be aware that this document has been compiled
by you under emotional stress. Also, be aware
that these documents are by definition colored
by your perceptions. But if you have done your
best to be honest and as objective as you
can be, it will prove an important first step
toward reconciliation.

# A Sanity Check

So here is what is next: you are going to test and refine the Love Resumes – with a little help from your friends. Obviously the harsh reality of getting over your ex is very tough. It is even tougher if you are doing it all alone. After the break-up there can be a little too much inner dialog. It is not unhealthy talking to yourself, but it is if you are fully obsessed over the break-up. You need somebody that you can vent with. That is just one of the many great things about having friends at a time such as this.

## CHOOSE THE RIGHT BUDDY

How to find the right buddy? Here are a few tips:
• Pick someone you trust and who knows you
• If possible, pick a buddy of the opposite sex. He or she probably is able to help you with the Venus & Mars-difficulties!
• Pick someone who dares to tell you the truth. It is not in your interest to talk to somebody who simply agrees with you. You need somebody who can give you his or her honest opinion, even if it is not so pleasant to hear... But you know: it takes a true friend to offer you tough love!

## BUDDY – THE INTERVIEW

While there is no right way to structure the interview with your buddies, the five interview questions below are probably useful because they are simple and have been tested successfully on many occasions.

A dinner or lunch is a good vehicle. You may also want to do it at your buddy's. Whatever is comfortable for the both of you: it is the result that matters.

### FIRST

Contact your buddy and schedule an appointment. Be sure to give a realistic estimate of how much time you will need and to explain why you want the appointment. Be open about the reason, being that you need help in order to get a better understanding of what went wrong in your relationship and that you want to receive open and honest feedback.

This may be of help in creating the change that may lead to winning your ex back. Finally, you may want to tell your buddy that the fact that you are making this request to him/her is no doubt a compliment. Because it is.

### SECOND

Identify general areas about which you want information as well as specific questions about which you would like to have answers. Define these by using your Love Résumé. Be sure to use both closed ended questions, such as 'how would you describe me' and open-ended questions, such as 'do you think it is true I am too selfish' and so forth.

This combination will help you to allow for unexpected insights and feedback yet keep the interview focused. See for a list of recommended interviews questions at the bottom of this page.

### THIRD
Conduct the interview. Now here is an issue: I am frequently asked about when to hand out a copy of your Love Résumé. So, what the best moment? I say: it depends. Some people prefer to use it as a 'pad' that provides guidance and makes cutting to the chase easier and less awkward. Others say that handing out the these documents early on is like asking a closed question and smothers open and creative feedback from your buddy. I usually propose a compromise: hand out the Love Résumé halfway the meeting or as much earlier as you would need in order to get you going.

Five questions you must ask your buddy:
1. Do you think that I have filled in my Love Résumé honestly? Why/Why not?

2. Do you think our relationship was good? Why/Why not?
3. Do you think I have been a good partner? Do you think my ex has been a good partner? Why/Why not?
4. Do you feel my ex and I have a chance to be back together? Why/Why not?
5. What, do you think, are the three most important things I should change to make the relationship better? What do you think my ex considers the most important things?

### SUZY AND MIKE
The whole thing about Mike's family had not come up until Ralph, buddy of Suzy answered question one with an honest 'no'. Apparently, Suzy had put this family issue totally away and had refrained from including it in her first version of her Love Résumé. This blunt 'no' was confronting at first but at the end of the meeting with Ralph, she could laugh about it. It had come to her as a relief in a funny way.

### FOURTH
Evaluate what you have learned. Write down the information given to you in some form that will be helpful to you later on. Be as specific as you can. Jot

down quotes. And be sure to make a note of what you did not find out: you may be more specific about this when you conduct your second interview.

## ARE YOU ABSOLUTELY SURE?

Hold on a second! You have done some hard work now, it has been a thorough and maybe painful examination. But what does it tell you? Are you still absolutely sure that you want your ex back? Or has it revealed that the break-up is for the better, that you both are better off without each other?

Think about it for a day and you should not be afraid of the outcome! It is really important to get this right. If it is going to lead to more misery, why bother getting your ex back. Fear of being alone, fear of never finding somebody else is a bad reason for getting back together with somebody.

As they say: better to turn back halfway than to get lost altogether and there is still a lot of work to be done. So, think again, are you sure? Are you willing to go through it? I know this is difficult. It is difficult to discern: do you miss your ex or do you miss the life the two of you had? Do you miss him or her or do you miss the comfort, the company, having somebody around? I know this sounds harsh, but it might be the true.

You are likely to remember the good points about your ex and forget the bad ones, that is how the human mind works: it tends to 'rehearse' the good points. It is a way for you to 'justify' the pain and hard work you are going through. This is called 'selective retention' and is used by marketers: they use drama and repetition in sending messages to their target customers.

Maybe you are deceiving yourself. Maybe your buddy can be a good help: he may want to remind you of the fact that you were not always happy with your ex when you were still together. Maybe it is your hurt pride talking. Or your rejected ego that wants to prove itself.

So do you really want to make up? Is it a relationship worth fighting for? Can you honestly say, that most days spent together were happy? Do you expect the same from life? Did you feel comfortable around each other?

If the outcome is that you are actually through with your ex, be glad: you can begin letting her go, start mourning and become a free man. If the outcome is that your relationship is worth fighting for, if you are convinced that something beautiful will come out, continue reading!

# you are perfect

within your imperfection

You want your ex back?

# step three

# preparing

3

# Like It Is
# New Year's...

By now you have finished your analysis of your love life so far, your relationship and interaction with your ex, and you have discussed it with your buddy. Out of all this, we are going to extract the things you might want to change, the actions you are going to take. In this chapter we are going to formulate your Relationship Resolutions.

# Relationship Resolutions

You cannot start a new relationship with your ex from where the old one ended. The end of a relationship is literal the death of it. The attraction and feelings you have for each other may still be the same but the relationship you had ended. And precisely because of that painful experience you are no longer the same people. The very experience of breaking-up changes who you are, who you think the other is and how you see reality.

Because you are no longer the same people, look at this experience as two new people, starting a new relationship together. You will find it much easier and you are more likely to get a more positive outcome if you give up the idea of trying to fix an old relationship and instead try to create a new and better one.

This is why formulating your Relationship Resolutions should be a treat. Think of it: you now have the opportunity to imagine how you would like things to be, how you would like to shape your life. This is your chance to create a new relationship, much better than the old one.

## HOW TO KEEP 'M

New Year's resolutions: a commitment that an individual makes to a project or the reforming of a habit, often a lifestyle change that is generally interpreted as advantageous. Some examples include resolutions to donate to the poor more often, to become more assertive, or to become more environmentally responsible, getting a better job, getting out of debt and saving money.

I guess that like most people you have made New Year's resolutions at some point in your life. Then you will probably know how difficult it is to keep them. Why? Because we are creatures of habit. Change is difficult.

How to keep your resolutions?
There are two basic rules that should help you:
1.  Don't set your goals too high.
2.  Make sure that you are passionate about the outcome.

Let your buddy help you setting your goals and break them down into small pieces and set a realistic timetable. Each time you achieve a milestone on the way to your resolutions, reward yourself. Buy yourself – or your buddy – a gift, for example.

Be persistent and make the changed lifestyle a new habit. If you consciously stay on track for three weeks,

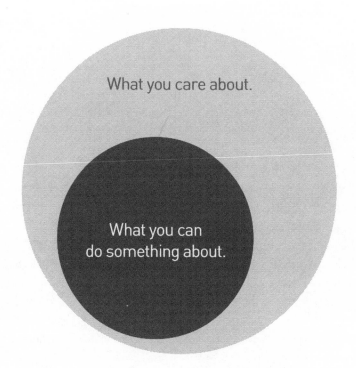

What you care about.

What you can
do something about.

*Circle of Influence*

chances are, staying the course will be much easier. Do your best not to fall off the wagon, but when you do, forgive yourself for being human and move on. We all experience failure in life. When this happens, learn from your failure. Ask yourself – what stopped you from doing what you said? Can you avoid that circumstance in the future?

To make realistic resolutions, you might want to look at the concept of circle of influence/circle of concern,

developed by Stephen Covey in his brilliant 'Seven Habits Of Highly Effective People':
The bigger circle is your circle of concern: it holds all the things that somehow concern you. Within this circle there is the circle of influence: holding all the things not only concerning you, but that you can control or can do something about. It is important to notice the difference and to accept what is beyond your reach, and at the same time try to enlarge your circle of influence.

## AN EXAMPLE:

In the case of Suzy and Mike, Suzy had to deal with Mike's cultural background. His family demanded a loyalty that got in the way of their relationship. Some of the things Mike's family wanted were totally beyond her influence. When I walked Suzy through the circle of influence, she eased down. It helped her to understand that elements outside her circle of influence were not to worry about, she said. And that the one to deal with was Mike, not so much his family.

## NOW MAKE THEM YOURSELF!

Now it is time you formulate your Relationship Resolutions that will result in a better relationship between you and your ex. Let your buddy help you. Here are some tips:

1. Your Relationship Resolutions should be realistic.
2. Make them short and formulate them positively ('I will do this from now on' instead of 'I won't do this anymore').
3. Visualise the outcome: try to see how you, your ex and your new relationship look, sound and even smell! This is a powerful tool, used by successful sportsmen.
4. In order to commit yourself truly: write them down and sign them with your buddy.

## RELATIONSHIP RESOLUTION EXAMPLE: SUZY

1. I will join a health club and go there at least twice a week.
2. I will be more open to Chinese culture and traditions. As a start, I will learn how to cook Chinese and better appreciate Chinese gastronomy, as of next week.
3. I will try to be less judgmental and show more understanding towards Mike's family.

## KEEP IN MIND: IT IS FLUID!

It is wonderful that you have produced your Relationship Resolutions, but bear in mind that you have produced them yourself: without the input from your ex yet. Chances are that when it comes to discussing your new relationship he or she might see things differently. That is why you should not regard your Relationship Resolutions as something fixed, but be prepared to make changes. How this is done without giving in you will learn in the next chapter.

# I'm gonna make him an offer

he cannot refuse

*Don Corleone – The Godfather*

# It Is Communication, Stupid!

By now you have thought of the relationship as
you would want it to be and you have formulated
your Relationship Resolutions. Ready to meet the
ex? Almost! In this part I would like to hand you
some important tools, all about communication.

# It's Not What You Say...

Because as you probably know: it is not what you say, it is how you say it. You may have come up with the best ideas in the world, if you are not able to convince the other, nobody's going to be interested. Look at business: you can have a great product, but if the salesperson is lousy, it is not going to work!

I would like to share with you two concepts that have been very useful for me over the years, in my professional and personal life. One is principled-negotiating, the other non-violent communication.

## PRINCIPLED NEGOTIATING

This is the situation: the relationship between you and your ex is not how you want it to be at the moment. You two have broken up, you want him or her back, while your ex doesn't. Now there is something to negotiate about. And with negotiation I mean two individuals communicating to find the best possible solution to an issue.

### NOT SOFT NOT HARD – THE 'THIRD WAY'

When in dilemma most people see two ways to negotiate: soft or hard. Fisher and Ury, two Harvard-professors, came up with a third way to negotiate: both soft and hard, a method of what they called 'principled negotiation'.

The key point is to decide issues on their merits. In this concept you and your ex are not opponents who both want the biggest slice of the pie, but you will try to find ways to enlarge the pie – together. Without giving in to pressure from the other side.

The grandmasters in this field are Roger Fisher and William Ury. They became famous because of their involvement to end the Iran hostage crisis, in '79. In Teheran fifty-two US citizens were held hostage at the US Embassy for 444 days by a group of Islamist students and militants.

Another historical feat was their contribution to the Camp David Accords in '78. At his summerhouse President Jimmy Carter arranged a historical peace treaty between two old archenemies, Israel and Egypt, using the techniques of Fisher and Ury.

Their work led eventually to the international best seller, Getting to YES.

# It's How You Say It!

## I SEE WHAT YOU DON'T SEE – PERCEPTIONS!

Imagine two people spending an entire day together. They work, have lunch, talk and laugh together. Now ask each of them what their day was like. Result? Their answers may be completely different. One has experienced a great day, while for the other it is been a drag. That is a matter of perspective and the same happens in relationships: two people develop their own set of perceptions of things that have happened.

Now take a step back and ask yourself: 'Have I ever tried to look at the situation from where my ex sits? Have I put myself in his/her shoes?' Perhaps not. Perhaps the first time you really did this was when you wrote the Love Résumé of your ex. In any case: most people don't. It may sound strange, but doing it is in your own interest! Let me explain why this notice of difference in viewpoint is so important. Ever heard of the glass half full, glass half empty?

## AN EXAMPLE – ASHLEY & DAVID

The case of Ashley and David is a good example. They held quite different perceptions towards their financial situation. And you know: they were both right!

Ashley was comfortable with the way things were going since their monthly household cost had stayed constant, allowing them to make trips to foreign countries, living a luxurious life.

David, however, was frustrated by the fact that his salary had hardly been raised in recent years. David thought of the neighbors on the right hand side, who made substantially more money.

Ashley compared their situation with the neighbors across the street, a family that had trouble making ends meet. David was making good money for the family. Ashley wished he would spend less time at the office.

It is about understanding each other's point of view. Try to feel what your partner feels or could feel. It won't hurt. It is not the same as agreeing to it.

## SO THIS IS WHAT YOU ARE SAYING?

So what went wrong with Ashley and David? They failed to explore the possibility of a difference in perceptions. They should have. It may be awkward, but it is worth more than the embarrassment.

It all starts by not blaming the other side for seeing things differently. The next step: communicate the message that:
- Both parties' perceptions can be right at the same time;
- you are prepared to carefully listen and to understand your ex's concerns and motivators; and that,
- you find these motivators and concerns important on your way to a solution.

So how do you show that you find these concerns important? That is easy. Just repeat what your ex says. For example: 'So you are saying...,' or 'Let me repeat this because I want to be sure I understand what you say.' You got the point: do not treat your ex's worries as unimportant. In addition, mind your body language, which is discussed in the next chapter.

Talk about each other's perceptions. Make sure that both parties are okay with the fact that perceptions may differ. Deal with it. Don't beat around the bush.

So what if your ex's perception is wrong? Or what if it is unfavorable to you? Then change the perception of the other side by looking for opportunities to act inconsistently with those perceptions. Likely the best way to do this is, is to make sure that the other side receives a message different from what it would expect from you, given his perceptions.

Sounds complicated? Let me give you a famous example, found in the book of Fisher and Ury. It goes back to '77 when the Israeli's saw Egypt and it is President Anwar Sadat as their enemy, who had made a surprise attack on Israel just a few years before. Sadat, who wanted peace, but who understood the Israeli's mistrusted him, decided to help alter that perception, by giving a message different from what the other party expected.

How? He flew to the capital of his enemies, Israel, Jerusalem. By making this surprise move, he showed himself a partner instead of an enemy. Sixteen months after Sadat's visit to Israel, the Israel-Egypt peace treaty was signed in Washington.

## NON-VIOLENT COMMUNICATION

Another useful tool I am about to show you is that of non-violent communication. Chances are big that you have noticed that you are emotional and easily upset these days. Perhaps you find you have become more defensive and have a greater temptation to retaliate in whatever situation.

This is not the optimal response, especially when communicating with your ex! You are aware of this, but how can you prevent it from happening? Let me introduce to you an exercise that was developed by Marshal Rosenberg. This famous psychologist is the creator of so-called non-violent communication. Ever heard of it? It is way of resolving conflicts and differences peacefully.

Basically, non-violent communication has four steps. These steps you got to remember every time you realize: 'Oh boy, here I go again, I am defending myself. I am about to retaliate, etc.'

### ONE: ARE YOU OBSERVING OR JUDGING?

Try not to interpret or judge. Stick to the facts, ask yourself: 'What has really happened?' So:

*'I saw you flirting with that woman'*
instead of
*'I saw that you were talking for an hour with that woman.'*
Lesson learned: if you feel you get emotional, stop for a second and remember the example: observation not interpretation.

### TWO: WHAT DO YOU FEEL?

What feelings do you get when you memorize a painful situation? Probably you will use words that relate to others. Perhaps you feel 'rejected' by your ex. You may feel this way, but the point of this second step is to try to avoid using words that relate to others. Other examples are: betrayed, manipulated. You get betrayed and manipulated by someone else, not by yourself!

If you use these kinds of verbs to talk about your feelings, you give others too much power over your emotions. So, stop describing yourself as a victim, in case you did. Take control of your emotions, do not blame others.

Lesson learned: try to use words that do not require the action of someone else. Only words that describe things for which you are responsible: like angry, afraid, happy, relaxed.

## BE CLEAR!

Communicate by clearly telling the other person what you need. Ask yourself: what do I need in this situation. In the example of David and Ashley, remember, in what way do you think Ashley should best communicate?

*'You work late five days a week.'*
or
*'I really feel the need to talk about your day with you when you come home.'*

## ASK – DON'T IMPOSE

This is the final step: when people have finally found out what they really want, they tend to be demanding instead of requesting.

Simple example:
*'Book these tickets!*
or
*'Would you mind booking these tickets?'*

What question is likely to generate a positive response?

Also, when making a request, be as specific as you can. By being more specific you increase chances. Practice these steps in everyday life and you will notice the difference: you will get better response. And that is your goal: getting a positive response from your ex.

any view
of things
that is not
strange

is false

*Neil Gaiman – The Sandman.*

# Make Room
# For Emotions

It is hard for me to judge, but you and your ex are probably more up for a battle than cooperatively working out solutions. Stakes are high – remember Maslov? – and you may both feel threatened. Emotions on one side may invoke new emotions on the other side – leading to a downward spiral away from finding a solution. Emotions may even bring the communication to an unwanted end.

# The Statisfaction Of Being Understood

So if you succeed in dealing with your emotions and managing those of your ex, your chances for success increase significantly. There are a couple of useful insights, developed by our friends Ury and Fisher.

Recognize and understand your emotions and those of your ex. Ask yourself: 'What is it I feel most emotional about?' Also try to imagine what would be the main emotions of your ex- you may want to check both your Love Resumes. Ury and Fisher even recommend writing down what your emotions – angry for instance, or worried and how you might like to feel – relaxed, perhaps confident.

When meeting your ex – we deal with that in the next chapter – it is important to make your emotions explicit and at the same time give room to your ex's. Be professional. Be prepared. The more you manage each other's emotions by acknowledging them as legitimate, the better chance you have they do not interfere with your strategy to win your ex back.

## LISTEN!

It is difficult to listen to others. Most people prefer being listened to. Listening is especially difficult in stressful situations. Example: most doctors repeat their advice more than once, because research has shown that patients, under stress caused by uncertainty, cannot reproduce what the doctor has just said. Even if it is as simple as: 'you're not allowed to eat salty food for a month.' This is why doctors write down their advice as well.

Now let us take this back to your situation: you must make sure that your ex understands what you say and that you understand what your ex says.

Business research has shown that active listening has two advantages. It enables you to understand the other side's perceptions, emotions, and what they try to say. At the same time, it improves what the other side says. This is because the other side will feel the satisfaction of being understood and heard. This will encourage them to communicate better.

Now, how do you make sure you are perceived an active listener? There are a number of ways to support this. Body language is obviously important. It is dealt with on page 84.

As said, another manner to show that you are listening actively is to occasionally rephrase 'Let me make sure I totally understand what you are saying because I feel it is important. Are you saying...?'. It is okay to even interrupt your ex for this. It shows that you are interested and motivated.

## TWO MORE USEFUL TECHNIQUES
### CREATE ALTERNATIVES

'The better your alternative, the greater your power'. This business saying may be confusing in the context of this book but there is a powerful lesson in it. It may or may not be applicable to your situation. It probably is. Here is the background.

Imagine you are in a salary negotiation. When are you most effective: if you had one or more job offers in your back pocket or if you had none? Now let us look at the perception of the other side. When would your potential employer be more inclined to make you an offer to you? Exactly: when they know you have some serious other options.

Now look at your situation. Ask yourself: do I have alternatives? Does my ex think I have alternatives? Does my ex have reason to believe I am in the market for other options?
Before we go to the question of what you can do to

improve your bargaining power and therefore your impact on your ex, please remember that pity or compassion is never a good reason to return to your partner. You do not want to reunite with your ex simply because your ex feels sorry for you. That is a weak basis.

So, what can you do to improve your alternatives? What can you do to make yourself more effective and create the impression that you have alternatives – remember the salary example?

What you want to do is start developing your alternatives. How to go about it? The best way to create alternatives for you is to go out and start dating other persons. How? We will deal with this later in this book.

One thing is for sure: someone who has options is more attractive in the eyes of the rest of the world. Work on it.

### MAKE IT EASY

You want your ex to give the two of you another chance. Now, take a step back and ask yourself: can I make the decision easier? In other words: how can I help my ex to make the decision I want her to make? Think about it this way: saying 'Yes' to your proposal should not be tough. It should be made as easy as possible. Provide answers to your ex. Not problems.

Here is a useful technique. People feel more comfortable making decisions if they aware of precedents. Use this. So look for ideas that your ex may have had in similar situations that support the decision you want from her. For instance: has your ex ever helped others to reconcile? Has she advised others to reconcile? Are you aware of friends or family of your ex that reconciled successfully? Perhaps you and your ex have made up before – successfully for a while.

Also, realize that your ex's decision of whether or not to come back to you, is likely to partially depend on the opinion of others: friends, family, neighbors and so forth. So picture your ex' inner circle and give your ex arguments to get approval, how to defend her decision to get back with you. Make sure your ex will be able to explain in simple terms what went wrong and how you both are going to solve it – this are basically your Relationship Resolutions. So it better be good.

## PRACTICE!

By now, you have armed yourself with a Relationship Resolutions, approved by your buddies, as well as several techniques to optimally communicate your Relationship Resolutions to your ex. You are aware that your Relationship Resolutions may take a different shape as a result of the feedback from your ex.

Finally, a simple word cloud to bring you in the mood for the meeting, to get the desired mind-set. I recommend looking at it a couple of times before you head off...

positive

humor empathic

listen alternatives

confident

You want your ex back?

# step four

# meeting

# At Last Boy Meets Girl

Okay, you are ready. You know what to do, you know what you woulld like to change. You know what to say to your ex and how to say it. It is time to meet your ex.

# Start: The Email

You are ready to get back in touch with your ex. How does it feel? Are you excited? I would be, I would be really excited to tell my ex about the past weeks, what I have discovered and learned about my resolutions, that I am ready to be back together and things will change – for the better.

But slow down. Take it easy. You don't know what the other side has been up to. Your ex surely has done some thinking, but you cannot tell how far he or she is in that process. You want to be with your ex, definitely talk to your ex, but maybe your ex is not ready for that. You have to be careful. The worst thing you can do now is scare him or her off. So don't show up unannounced at your ex' home or work. Also, do not call your ex. Not as a first step.

The best way to get back in touch again is through email. Even better, how old-fashioned it may seem, is a letter. This is romantic and everybody, male or female still loves to receive a real letter.
Why write? For several reasons. First of all writing forces you to really think about what you want to say and this is crucial in this phase. Secondly it gives you the opportunity to say what you want exactly without having to deal with your ex responding immediately: it is one-way communication. Thirdly, it is not aggressive. Your ex can read the mail in his or her own time and space, reread it probably two or three times.

Once you have written your mail, my advice is to sleep on it. What seemed to be a brilliant letter yesterday, may turn out to be a bad idea the next morning... When you write your ex an email, send it to his or her personal mail account, not the business one, even if you normally used the business account: you just don't want to take the risk of annoying your ex. Also think about the probable time your ex is going to receive it. If you know that on Saturday mornings he is always busy for example, wait until the afternoon. Of course this doesn't count when you leave the delivery to the postman!

## EXAMPLES

Now, what to write? Of course this is a personal matter and you know your ex best. An important advice is: 'BU!' Like Billy Joel sang 'Don't go changing, to try and to please me.' If you always call your ex 'honey', stick to that.

But some things need to be said and some lines in a certain priority always work. Therefore it might be useful to look at the following example, an email written by Ashley to her ex, David:

*Dear David,*

*How are you? I hope you are fine! How is work? Did you manage to get the assignment you were waiting for?*
*Or*
*Was your evaluation as good as you hoped? I am sure it was: you have done really well for the company the last couple of months! (Show interest in your ex first.)*
*I have done a lot of thinking since we broke up. I think that despite our differences our relationship could really work.*

*(Let your ex know, that he or she has been on your mind.)*
*I would like us to meet and see how we are doing. Shall we have lunch next Saturday, at Carol's Corner? I believe they still have the best strawberry shakes in town! (Suggest a lunch date – more about that later. And show you want it to be a cheerful meeting!)*

The pattern you will recognize from this example is I.T.P.:
'**I**' stands for showing interest. This interest underlines that you and your ex know each other and that you care about how your ex is currently doing.
'**T**' stands for thinking. By communicating that you have been 'thinking', you send the message that you want to reach out, you are open to learn from mistakes you have made. In short, you position yourself as a good listener who, as we have seen before.
'**P**' stands for proposal. This proposal must be clear. Say what you want, remember? The proposal of Ashley is a good example: 'lunch next Saturday, at Carol's Corner'. Much better than 'Do you want to hang out and do something next weekend?' – that is too vague.

So remember: ITP. It will work.

# And Then: The Call

You have sent an email, now you first have to wait for your ex to answer. But for how long? Again: do not rush! You have written important things, give your ex some time to digest all this, to make up her or his mind. Wait at least five days.

There are three possibilities: your ex wants to meet you. In that case, skip this part about the call and continue reading at Meeting Preparation on the next page. Two: your ex replies your email, explaining he or she

doesn't want to see you, or three: your ex does not reply. If that is the case, you are going to call your ex.

The key-thing is to prepare this call thoroughly. First of all think of the best time to call: try to think of your ex's schedule: don't call when you know your ex is probably at work, at his mother's, having his usual bowling night out with his buddies.

You may be nervous for this call – that is normal. But try to be calm, think of ways to relax before the call. Maybe it helps to go out for a walk first, listen to a song that you like, call a friend. It is important that you try to show as little desperation as possible in the call.

First talk casually, for example ask how you are ex is doing, talk about a television program you both like or something positive that has happened to a mutual friend. Make it nice and friendly, try to ease your ex: keep in mind that it is probably as difficult for him or her to talk to you as it is for you!

You should make the phone call, short and sweet. Do not rush off the phone, but gently guide the conversation to a quick end. In this first call, beware to bring up the nasty stuff. Do not mention ugly memories, don't go into the reasons for your break-up: this is not time for that. Keep things light.

First get used to each other, get comfortable again – not just you, but notice that this is something difficult for your ex as well. Once the conversation is okay, you can mention the email and ask your ex to meet with you.

Where and how shall you meet? Coffee or a short lunch is perfect, because there are time limits involved. You want enough time to talk to each other, but you don't want to prolong it. You want to just give them a taste of the 'new' you. Propose a date that is about four to five days ahead so you will have time to prepare for the meeting.

Then there is always a chance that you receive the answer you don't want to hear: 'no'. Your ex probably won't say it directly: it will sound like 'well, I don't know' or 'I am not sure that is such a good idea'. Do not panic! Be cool, and most of all: never beg or plead!

Begging will give your ex the upper hand. Try to stay on the same level, try to remain equal partners, even though it feels as though your ex has just rejected you. Try to say something like 'Yes, you're right. Knowing you I guess it would be wiser not to see each other now, I feel the same.'

Pleading only reduces your chances. Your ex might say 'yes', but only out of pity, and that will never lead to you winning back your ex. Even worse in this situation is to get angry or argumentative. You don't want it to become a point!

The trick is to handle the rejection with class and grace. It is the only solution: just wish your ex well, friendly, casually changing the subject. It proves how calm you are, how respectful you were towards your ex and this will interest him or her. Maybe not ready to meet you yet, but if he or she is, your ex will surely remember the way you handled this.

After the conversation is over your ex will have time to digest the call. He or she will realize 'Wow! This is not the same person I remember when we broke up'. When you show confidence and politeness, it will have a positive effect, whether you think it will or not. So, believe me, you should not be surprised if your ex calls you back, some time later: 'no' doesn't mean a 'no' forever!

Even if you never do, it is okay. Hopefully, you are in such a better place, that you will be fine with it. Sure, you may be disappointed, but you know you gave it your best, and you handled the whole situation with a lot of class. You can feel very proud of yourself.

OH NO: VOICE-MAIL!

There is of course the possibility that you get your ex's voice-mail. What to do? Like James Hightower in 'Winning Back Your Ex', I advice you not to leave a message, because you want to talk to him or her directly. Even if your ex has caller ID and can find out that you called, it is okay. Your ex will see that you have called and return the call or he or she will ignore it.

Let us look at the latter situation: your ex ignores you. Be cool about it, don't panic, don't even think of calling your ex every ten minutes from now on. If your ex returns the call: great. If not, no big deal. Wait for a couple of days and then call again. Nobody likes to wait, but these days won't be the end of the world.

Your ex may ignore your second call, again wait for a couple of days, and call again, never leaving a message. You know what it does to your ex? If you don't rush, don't push, your ex will feel that you are calm. It makes a good impression and moreover: if there is enough time between the calls, it raises your ex's curiosity. He or she wants to know why you are calling.

Meanwhile, have fun! Do not sit and wait for the phone to ring. Go out and have fun, go out on dates, take good care of yourself. If a few weeks pass by without a sign of life from your ex, then it is about time to face reality. Sad but true, you have to let go, you and your ex were not meant to be.

# make things

## as simple as

# possible

but no simpler

*Albert Einstein*

# Be The Best You

When the two of you were in love you looked
your best: you were in great shape, dressed
sharp, you took good care of yourself. Hopefully
you have followed the advice I mentioned earlier
in the book and have begun to be become the
Best You again.

# A Few Facts On Presentation

What to wear? This is important. You have got to feel good and confident and your clothes can help you! I advise you a combination of old & new: wear the shirt (or pants) you feel really good in and combine them with a new item, something that would impress your ex. Something you are pretty sure of you are ex would want you to wear, that he or she mentioned once. But again: 'BU'!

Also: pay attention to the way you smell. I am talking about your fragrance. Do not underestimate the power of flavours and scents: I advise you to use the same fragrance you wore when the two of you first kissed – if you can still remember of course! It works on an unconscious level and will remind your ex of that happy time.

## BODY LANGUAGE

Be aware of body language. Use it. The impact is huge when applied well. If, on the other hand, you do not control it, the impact is disastrous. It is said that body language conveys more than seventy percent of information of an individual's character, power, and trustworthiness and you do not need a trained eye to notice.

How much information people give off by non-verbal communication is totally underestimated. Flipside is that here is a clear opportunity to read what your ex feels so that you can respond to this and improve the communication.

DO'S

WHEN YOU ENTER THE ROOM IF YOU ARE COMFORTABLE YOU SHOW

**Firm handshake:** shows self-confidence.
**Smiling eyes and relaxed brows:** comfortable.
**Direct eye contact:** likes you, interested.
**Eyes open slightly more than usual:** gives people a welcome impression.

WHEN YOU SIT DOWN

**Open hands:** trust in other and an interest in their opinions. It also offers an opinion and invites the sharing of the other person's view.
**Fingers interlocked placed behind the head leaving elbows open and armpits exposed:** feeling comfortable.
**Legs wide apart or sitting straddle-legged:** shows that a person is feeling safe, and is self-confident. Can also show leadership.
**Crossed legs with highest foot in the direction of the speaker:** relaxed and self-confident and they are listening very carefully.
**Mirroring you:** likes you, wants to be friendly.

## ACTIVE LISTENING

**Fingers interlocked placed behind the head leaving elbows open and armpits exposed:** very open to ideas.

**Leaning forward:** interested.

**Slowly nodding:** shows interest and validates the interviewer, and this subtly encourages him to continue.

**Still:** more interested in what you are saying than anything.

## PHYSICAL ATTRACTION

**Dangling the loose shoe from the toes:** signals physical attraction.

## DON'T-S:
## NERVOUSNESS EN TENSE

**Bitten your fingernails:** nervousness.

**Wring your hands:** nervousness.

**Twisting the feet continuously:** a person is nervous or concerned.

**Cleared your throat:** nervousness.

**Rigid body posture:** anxious, uptight.

**Weak hand shake:** nervous, shy, insecure, or afraid of interaction.

## BE INSECURE

**Adjusting your tie:** insecurity.

**Biting the lips:** expresses embarrassment and lack of self-confidence.

**Shoulders hunched forward:** lacking interest or feeling inferior.

**Clinging hands:** clinging to objects, such as bags, chairs, tables show a need for support, so confusion or insecurity.

**Arms crossed:** cautious and defensive.

## WHEN YOU ARE NOT BEING ON THE SAME LEVEL

**Pressed lips/pursed lips:** convey disagreement and disapproval. It communicates a desire to end the discussion.

**Resting chin on palm:** critical, negative towards the other individual.

**Limited or no eye contact:** lying, uninterested, uncomfortable.

## BEING NOT SUCH A GOOD LISTENER

**Rapidly nodding your head:** shows impatient and eager to add something to the conversation.

## ANNOYED

**Retracted shoulders:** suppressed anger.

**Nose-rubbing or nose-touching:** a sign of doubt, it often reveals a negative reaction.

**Tension in brow:** confusion, tension, fear.

**Raised chin:** implies aggression that may be acted on if the conversation is not ended.

**Tapping fingers:** agitated, bored.

## NOT BEING OPEN

**A big smile that goes on longer and disappears slower:** unreal or fake smile.

**Fidgeting with hands or objects (for example, with a pencil):** bored or has something to say.

**Holding the hand before the mouth:** hiding something.

**Covered hands:** raising the back of one or both hands against others indicates keeping of distance and concealing feelings.

If you want to read more about this subject, I recommend you 'The Definitive Book of Body Language' by Allan & Barbara Pease.

# Live is lived forward

## and understood backward!

# The Meeting

First of all: have fun! Enjoy the date. It is great
to see your ex again, you look good, you are well
prepared, you have some nice things to talk
about, you feel better now: it is been a month
or so since you last met, so be cool. And be
confident. This is what will attract your ex
the most: confidence is sexy and powerful.
Wait a second, you say. I am not so sure about
this! I am nervous; I am not so cool!

# Confidence Is Sexy

What to do? Well. Whatever you do, be yourself. Don't try to act confidence, that does not work, especially not with your ex: few people know you better than your ex, he or she will look right through you.

So this confidence has got to be true. Let me help with some advice that might help you. First of all: don't regard the date as a favour from your ex. You want to enter the date as equal partners, you want to explore if reconciliation is an option – that should be your state of mind. Another aspect that will increase your confidence is to have alternatives. Be careful when mentioning them (him or her) though – do it subtly, not in a bragging way, that might hurt your ex. But it works: if you tell someone that he can have everything but the apple-pie, he wants the pie... Be the pie.

You are partners in this process, both looking for ways to enlarge the pie remember. Being partners, not opponents, you make sure that you don't sit across from each other, but right-angled or –even better- next to each other.

What to talk about? First you make sure you two are comfortable, just as you did during the phone conversation. At a certain moment, you know best yourself, it is time to mention the break-up. You can ask your ex how he or she feels, be empathic, remember the lessons you have learned. Try to listen well. Let him get it off of his chest, let your ex finish, don't start blaming, even though your ex might be blaming you. Swallow your pride, bite your tongue, but don't react.

Then you want to tell your ex how you have been doing. You want to share your Relationship Resolutions, your thoughts about how you see the relationship work. You can be proud of all the work you have done, but don't be disappointed if your ex doesn't agree right away. Remember: it is fluid, you have thought this out without the input of your ex.

What if you are ex is seeing somebody else? This is not a nice thing to hear, especially when you hear about this for the first time during your date. But still, don't let it get you down. Have faith and be confident. The chances are big that this new person is a rebound-lover, something your ex might need. Don't bother your ex about this, don't argue, but be her friend – be above it.

Another thing that you might want to try, if things are going well, is to break the touch barrier. Be careful, subtle and not aggressive. And creative. Maybe you want to adjust the collar of your ex's shirt or touch her hair slightly because you say there is something in it – even when that is not the case. It will show you where you stand: if your ex reacts smilingly, it is great. If your ex shows that he or she is uncomfortable with it, that is a pity, but it means you have a way to go – no big deal.

## ENDING THE DATE

Okay, the date is over, your time is up. You both have to go back to work, friends or whatever. How to end it? This can be pretty awkward. Here is some advice:

- Try to end the date on a peak: when you have just said something funny that has made your ex laugh, for example.
- Don't ask your ex out on another date, immediately – even if the date has been great. Wait! But if your ex proposes another date, of course you can accept it.
- Don't leave all happy and cheery, try to remain cool. Why? You don't want to give the impression that you are completely satisfied with the outcome – that is also negotiating.

## THE SECOND DATE

What to do after the first date? Wait first. Don't rush. Give your ex the time to reflect, don't be pushy. Wait. Maybe it is your ex who calls first – that is good news (unless of course it is to say that he or she never wants to see you again). But if not, wait a week and call then, casually and friendly. And when the moment is there, during this conversation, suggest a second date.

The first date was to get in touch, to know how the other was doing, the second date has a different nature. This time you want a bonding experience, something fun. This time you could meet at night, maybe for dinner and a movie. Or you meet in the daytime and do something active, go for a ride, maybe some golf or whatever are the things the two of you like. You might even want to go a little further and plan something you know your ex really wants to do, something adventurous like bungee jumping, to name something crazy. Going out on an active date has a great advantage: it is a perfect way to create new mutual experiences.

I guess you get the point by now. Have fun, talk when you feel it is called for and gradually you will grow together – if all goes well to a new and better relationship!

# Sex

A delicate issue and dealt well with by James
Hightower in his excellent book 'Winning Back
Your Ex'. If things are going well with the two
of you, then obviously there is going to be some
sexual tension. It may not be stated, but it is in
the back of both of your minds. You both know
what could happen. How to deal with it?
That depends if you are a man or a woman.

# If You Are A Man

A man wants to restart having sex with his ex as quickly as possible. But keep in mind: in general women are more serious about sex than men. If a girl agrees to sleep with her ex-boyfriend she feels that they are back together. For a woman, having sex with her ex is a lot easier than sleeping with a man she has not slept with before.

I guess you might be a little nervous about this. Although you have slept with your ex innumerable nights, this is a big thing. How does it work, what are the do's en don't-s when it comes to sleeping with your ex? First of all, a very practical one: perhaps needless to say, but if you invite her to your house, make sure your house is clean. What should be the reason to invite her? Anything goes. Just come up with something. It can be a new CD you want her to listen to. Just make sure it sounds acceptable, although she of course already knows what is going on.

It is important that you don't ask her. The reason is that if it is a question she has the option to refuse, because she feels she has to. But when you phrase it as a statement, you don't allow her to feel guilty for saying 'yes'. Still, it is up to her: if she says 'no' you know that you two are not as far as you

had hoped. Respect that! Remember the phone-routine: don't argue, don't beg. Just give her a little time.

Once you are in your place, take it easy. Play the CD, or whatever excuse you have come up with and then carefully try to touch her, her hand maybe, almost accidental, and see what happens. Her response will tell you if you can move on or stop right there. Don't be aggressive, always respect her wishes, even it that means that you won't end up in bed together. Take it easy: if it doesn't happen this time, wait a little longer. Nothing to worry about – you are doing fine.

# If You Are A Woman

It is different for a woman. A woman, in general, will only sleep with her ex if she senses that there is full commitment. Remember: you are in charge! Men are hunters and appreciate a difficult sexual conquest. So make them work for it, not the first time, even if you feel like it, do not give in easily!

By doing this you are adding a much-needed desire that was obviously missing from the original relationship. Remember how I said, you are going to try to make it as exciting as it was when you first met. Well, this is a sure fire way to do it. It has an important side effect: it increases his respect for you!

# Back Together!

Congratulations, you are back together! Enjoy
and relax, but remember: love is a verb... Now all
seems perfect again, but you two should not take
things for granted. You two need to work to on
your relationship. At this moment it is still fragile
and you have to make it stronger, strong enough
to withstand the difficulties that will certainly be
there some day.

# Love Is A Verb...

In this book I have used business concepts in order
to improve your personal life. Let me end in style by
using one of Stephen Covey again, comparing your
relationship to a bank account. You and your partner
share an account, a Relationship bank account. It
holds the amount of trust that is been built between
the two of you. In the beginning the account is empty
and you fill it by making deposits: being honest,
keeping promises, showing respect and commitment.

When the account is low you have to be careful.
There is tension and suspicion, it may feel like you
are walking on a minefield. When on the other hand
the account is high, things go well. Communication
is easy, you give each other some slack. You two are
allowed to make a mistake, there is room to make
a withdrawal from this account. So, keep making
deposits. As I said: love is a verb...

keep in mind

# love
## is a
## verb

# When Your Ex Does Not Want You Back?

Maybe the two of you don't hit it off the way you would have hoped. Then what? Maybe you end up having the same quarrels as when you were together. Don't panic. It is too early to write the thing off. Give it a little more time. You both have to get used to a new situation. It is difficult to change the old dynamics.

# Going On With Your Life

If however, after a couple of dates, things don't improve, you might want to doubt the relationship. Maybe it was not meant to be after all.

Or maybe you did not manage to meet with your ex. That is sad, but it happens. If you have done your best, tried everything you could using the tools you have learned and still it has not worked: give it up. But as I said before, that doesn't mean you are going to be alone for the rest of your life.

How can you tell it is really over? I have to admit that I don't have an answer to that. You have to rely on your own deeper wisdom, your intuition. I can only advise you to let go, try to go out on dates and have fun and time will tell. It helps to change your mind-set here: your ex is not the only person in the world you could have a relationship with! There are so many others, different than your ex, but once you manage to open yourself to new people you might see new ways.

Letting go of a relationship can be tough, especially if you have worked so hard to make it work – I know. Again, use your buddies and friends, they can help

you to accepting the fact that you and your ex are not going to become lovers again. It is a process of mourning, like you do when you have lost a beloved one – though your ex is still around and you will become friends instead of lovers.

It will be sad, but hey, that is life and I promise you: there will be bad days too, but gradually you will feel better. I advise you to keep up the good work, keep visiting your health club, mind what you eat and do all those other things I have shown you in the beginning of this book. Keep going on dates, have fun, try to meet new people, how difficult this may be.

Has all the hard work, the talks with your buddies, the Love Résumé, reading this book, been for nothing? Of course not. Think of it this way: it has helped to know yourself a little better and hopefully you have learned from the tools I have tried to hand you. It has made you a wiser and more balanced person, better equipped for a next relationship. And besides, being able to negotiate and to communicate well is always valuable, in your personal and your professional life!

## CREATE ALTERNATIVES: START DATING

It is important to have alternatives, I showed you earlier in the book. It will boost your self worth and confidence. How? Go out on a date! Where to find one? Well, there are potential dates everywhere. Maybe there is somebody you wanted to ask for years, a guy you noticed in your health club or the girl from the coffee shop.

I realize, for many people it is not that easy. But nowadays there is a great solution: internet dating. It may not sound very romantic, but millions and millions use it and have found a partner online. There are many dating sites, like match.com, friendfinder.com, chemistry.com, to mention a few. Google 'dating site' and you will see more.

There are many good things about internet dating. First of all you have got loads and loads of people to choose from. You can pick your criteria and select on age, length, color of hair, education, religion: whatever! It is easy to get in touch, you just have to email and take it from there.

When you have a date, prepare it the same we discussed in a couple of pages earlier: dress well and be confident. Also, keep in mind that this new date is probably not your future wife. That is not what this is about. You just want to have a nice time with somebody and take your mind off your ex, and as a bonus, make him or her a little jealous.

And yes, of course he or she is different than your ex. But there is one mistake that you do not want to make: talk all night about your ex. If the subject comes to your ex, answer shortly and then politely change the conversation. This is a date, not a talk with your buddy. Focus on your date: all the tools you have learned are useful here. So try to listen, mind your body language.

If you start comparing this date to your ex, don't worry. That is natural. Let it happen. Accept it. If this date doesn't work out, don't take it personal, even though your ego has had a blow because of the break-up.

Made in the USA
San Bernardino, CA
12 December 2019

61266165R10066